910.91634 Stewart
Titanic

WITHDRAWN

04/10/2012

W9-BKY-244

Titanic

Melissa Stewart

NATIONAL GEOGRAPHIC

Washington, D.C.

For Gerard, who sails with me through
rough waters as well as smooth seas

—M.S.

Copyright © 2012 National Geographic Society
Published by the National Geographic Society, Washington, D.C. 20036. All rights reserved.
Reproduction in whole or in part without written permission of the publisher is strictly prohibited.

Design by YAY! Design

Paperback ISBN: 978-1-4263-1059-1   Library ISBN: 978-1-4263-1060-7

There are three main kinds of artwork in this book. Recent color photographs show Bob Ballard's team at work and artifacts recovered from the ship since 1985. Black-and-white historical images were taken around the time *Titanic* sank. A bit of color has been added to some of these photos. Many of the most dramatic images in this book are extremely realistic color paintings by artist Ken Marschall. Mr. Marschall is one of the world's leading experts on the ship and the events surrounding its sinking. He has been painting scenes of *Titanic* for more than 40 years and has visited the shipwreck twice.

Photo Credits: Cover, Raymond Wong/National Geographic Stock; 1, akg-images; 2, Computer Earth/Shutterstock; 4-5, Ken Marschall; 6 and 7 (top) Emory Kristof/National Geographic Stock; 7 (bottom), Cynthia Johnson/Getty Images; 8 (top left), public domain; 8 (top right), Mary Evans Picture Library; 8 (bottom), Universal Images Group/Getty Images; 9, 10-11, Ken Marschall; 12 (top left), Ken Marschall; 12 (center left), Hulton-Deutsch Collection/Corbis; 12 (bottom left), public domain; 12 (top right), SSPL/Getty Images; 12 (center right), prism68/Shutterstock; 12 (bottom right), Universal Images Gr/akg-images; 12-13 (background), Rich Carey/Shutterstock; 13 (top left), BlueMoon Stock/Superstock; 13 (center left), Topical Press Agency/Getty Images; 13 (top right), Ken Marschall; 13 (center right), Zayats Svetlana/Shutterstock; 13 (bottom), IvicaNS/Shutterstock; 14, Mary Evans Picture Library/ONSLO; 15 (top), Underwood & Underwood/Corbis; 15 (center and bottom), Mary Evans Picture Library; 16-17, Ken Marschall; 17 (top and center), Bettmann/Corbis; 17 (bottom), Mary Evans Picture Library; 18, akg-images; 19, Paul Souders/Getty Images; 20 and 21 (top), Mary Evans Picture Library; 21 (bottom) and 22-23, 25, Ken Marschall; 26, Father Browne/Universal Images Group/Getty Images; 27 and 28, Ken Marschall; 29, Straus Historical Society; 30-31, Ken Marschall; 32 (top), National Archives and Records Administration; 32 (bottom), National Archives/Mary Evans Picture Library; 33, The Image Works/akg-images; 34 (top), Bettmann/Corbis; 34 (bottom), Time Life Pictures/Mansell/Time Life Pictures/Getty Images; 34-35 (background), SSPL/Getty Images; 35 (left), Alexander Feldmann/Corbis; 35 (right), National Maritime Museum, London/The Image Works; 36 (top), Topical Press Agency/Getty Images; 36 (bottom left), Bettmann/Corbis; 36 (bottom center), celebrity/Alamy; 36 (bottom right), *Titanic* Images/Universal Images Group/SuperStock; 37, 20th Century Fox/Paramount/The Kobal Collection/Art Resource, NY; 38, 40-41, Ken Marschall; 42 (top left), Mary Evans Picture Library; 42 (top right), Bruce Dale/National Geographic Stock; 42 (bottom), Ralph White/Corbis; 43, Emory Kristof/National Geographic Stock; 44, Brennan Phillips/Woods Hole Oceanographic Institute; 45 (top and bottom inset), Emory Kristof/National Geographic Stock; 45, Matthew Polak/Sygma/Corbis; 46 (top), FM Browne SJ/Davison & Associates Ltd/Getty Images; 46 (center left), Paul Souders/Getty Images; 46 (bottom left and center right), Ken Marschall; 46 (bottom right), Emory Kristof/National Geographic Stock; 47 (top left and top right), Ken Marschall; 47 (center left and bottom left), Bettmann/Corbis; 47 (center right), Ken Marschall; 47 (bottom right), Mary Evans Picture Library.

Printed in the United States of America

12/WOR/1

Table of Contents

Shipwrecks and Sunken Treasure

Illustration of *Titanic* shipwreck, 1985

Ever dreamed of exploring the ocean for a shipwreck? Imagine how exciting it would be to discover a hidden treasure.

Think that kind of thing only happens in the movies? Think again. In 1985, Robert Ballard led a team that discovered a sunken ship called R.M.S. *Titanic*.

Other people have found shipwrecks. But *Titanic* is special. It's one of the most famous ships of all time.

The whole world was excited about Ballard's discovery.

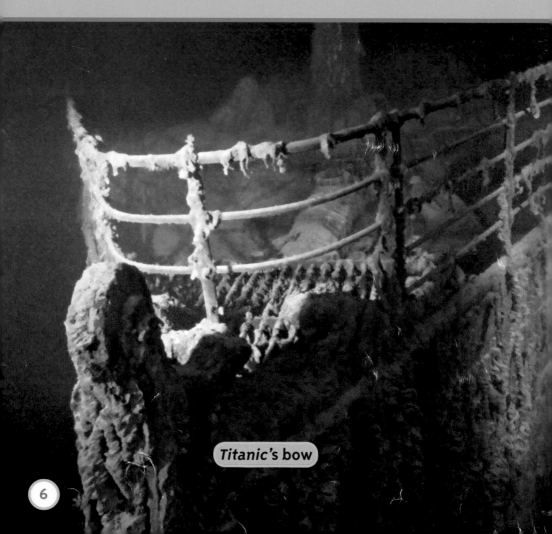

Titanic's bow

Robert Ballard and his crew celebrate on board their research ship, the *Knorr*, after they first spotted wreckage from *Titanic* in 1985.

In His Own Words

"My team had been watching the ocean floor with an underwater camera for days—and all we'd seen was mud. Late one evening, our camera suddenly passed over a ship's boiler . . . and at that moment, we knew . . . we'd found it."

—*Robert Ballard*

The Wonder Ship

What made *Titanic* so special? In 1912, it was the biggest ship ever built. That's why some people called it the "wonder ship."

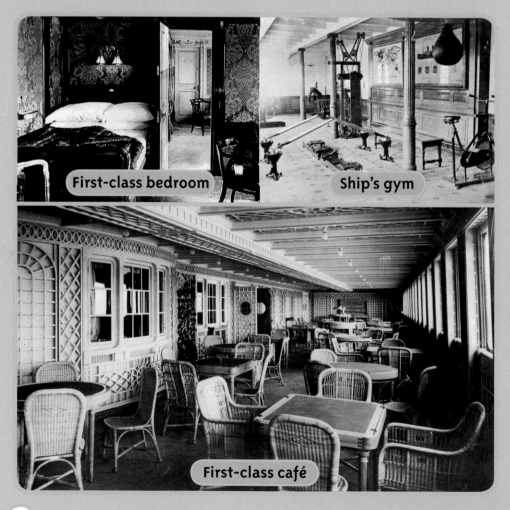

First-class bedroom

Ship's gym

First-class café

Grand staircase

Other people called it a "floating palace."
Titanic had every possible luxury—fine wood
paneling, crystal and gold light fixtures, and a
grand staircase with a skylight above it.

First-class passengers
ate fancy meals
and enjoyed the
ship's gym and
swimming pool.

Titanic Terms

LUXURY: Something that
offers pleasure or comfort,
but isn't necessary; often
difficult or expensive to get

Titanic Terms

BOW: The front end of a ship

STERN: The back end of a ship

HULL: The lowest part of a ship, partly covered with water

Titanic had nine decks, or levels, with separate areas for first-class, second-class, and third-class passengers.

Smokestack

Stern

Hull

Third-class cabin

Second-class cabin

In Her Own Words

"My pretty little cabin with its electric heater and pink curtains delighted me. Its beautiful lace quilt, and pink cushions, and photographs all around— it all looked so homey."

—*First-class passenger Lady Duff Gordon*

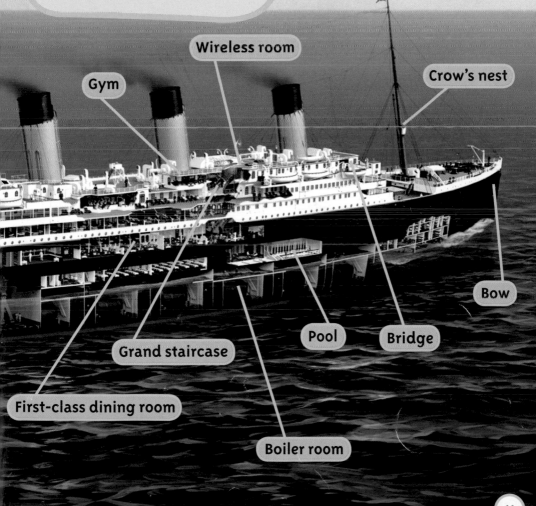

Wireless room

Gym

Crow's nest

Bow

Grand staircase

Pool

Bridge

First-class dining room

Boiler room

10
Cool Things
About
Titanic

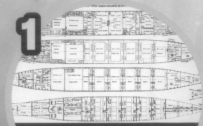

1

Titanic was almost as long as three football fields.

2

Including the four smoke-stacks, the ship was as tall as a 17-story building.

3

Titanic's engines used more than 800 tons of coal each day. The ship's top speed was 24 knots (27 miles an hour).

4

Titanic was one of the first ships to have a telephone system and electric lights in all the rooms.

5

The ship had four elevators, a heated swimming pool, a gym, two libraries, and two barber shops.

6

Each day, the passengers and crew used 14,000 gallons of drinking water.

7

Smoke and steam made by *Titanic*'s boilers escaped through three stacks. Builders added a fourth stack because they thought it made the ship look better.

8

Titanic could carry 3,547 passengers and crew. About 2,200 people traveled on its first voyage.

9

Some passengers paid about $99,000 in today's money to travel aboard *Titanic*.

10

To feed the passengers and crew, *Titanic* had 86,000 pounds of meat, 40,000 eggs, 40 tons of potatoes, 7,000 heads of lettuce, 3,500 pounds of onions, 36,000 apples, and 1,000 loaves of bread on board.

Building Titanic

WHITE STAR
ROYAL MAIL STEAMER
"TITANIC"

Titanic being built in Ireland, 1910

Titanic Terms
TRAGIC: Sad, dreadful, disastrous

Titanic's tragic story began in 1907. That's when J. Bruce Ismay of the British shipping company White Star Line and William J. Pirrie of Harland and Wolff shipyards decided to build three huge ships. One of those ships was *Titanic*.

J. Bruce Ismay, Chairman, White Star Line

In 1909, Thomas Andrews began work on *Titanic* in Belfast, Ireland. The ship was finished on March 31, 1912.

Lord William J. Pirrie, Chairman, Harland and Wolff

In early April, *Titanic* arrived in Southampton, England. Then a 900-person crew took a week to prepare for the ship's first voyage.

Thomas Andrews, Managing Director, Harland and Wolff

Bon Voyage

Illustration of *Titanic* docked at Southampton, England

Col. John Jacob Astor, IV, real estate millionaire from New York

Benjamin Guggenheim, who made his fortune in the mining business

Isidor Straus, owner of Macy's department store

When *Titanic* left England on April 10, 1912, it had an impressive list of passengers. White Star Line's chairman, J. Bruce Ismay, and *Titanic* builder Thomas Andrews were on board. So were some of the richest people in the world.

The ship also carried many middle-class passengers and poor immigrants who hoped for a better life in America.

Titanic Terms

IMMIGRANTS: People who leave one country to settle in another country

For the first few days of the trip, passengers felt like they were on vacation. They spent their time strolling around the deck, playing cards, and enjoying the ship's fine food and other luxuries.

But all that changed on Sunday, April 14, 1912. That's when *Titanic* entered an area of the North Atlantic Ocean known as Iceberg Alley.

Passengers strolling the deck of *Titanic*

Most of an iceberg's bulk is located below the ocean's surface. That makes it hard for sailors to know how big the icy chunk really is.

weird but true

Titanic Terms
ICEBERG: A large mass of ice floating in the sea

Tragedy at Sea

As *Titanic* cruised across the wavy water at top speed, it received nine ice warnings from other ships. But wireless operators Jack Phillips and Harold Bride were busy sending and receiving messages from passengers. They didn't deliver all the warnings to the bridge.

Titanic Terms

BRIDGE: A ship's control center. *Titanic* was steered and navigated from its bridge.

WIRELESS: An early form of radio that relayed messages through a coded series of beeps.

Wireless room similar to the one on *Titanic*

Captain Edward J. Smith seemed to ignore the messages he did receive during the day. Before dinner, he finally changed the ship's course to the south. But he didn't slow down.

Captain Smith had a long, successful career at sea. Commanding *Titanic* was supposed to be his last assignment before retiring. But he went down with his ship.

After sunset, stars shone brightly in the moonless sky. The air was bitterly cold, and the water was glassy smooth.

Just before midnight, Frederick Fleet, one of the ship's lookouts, spotted a large, dark object in the water.

weird but true

Many people believed *Titanic* was unsinkable, but the builders never made that claim.

He rang the alarm bell three times and shouted, "Iceberg right ahead."

First Officer William Murdoch reacted quickly. He ordered the crew to reverse the engines and turn the boat left, away from the iceberg. Then he pulled a switch to close the bulkheads.

But it was too late.

Titanic Terms

BULKHEADS: Walls meant to slow or prevent flooding by separating *Titanic*'s hull into 16 separate compartments

Most of the passengers were asleep. They didn't even feel the iceberg scrape the side of the ship. But the damage was done.

Captain Smith and Thomas Andrews rushed below decks. When Andrews saw how much seawater was gushing into the ship, he estimated *Titanic* would sink in less than two hours.

DOOMED!

Within ten minutes of the collision, *Titanic's* five front compartments were flooded to a depth of fourteen feet. *Titanic's* hull had sixteen compartments. The ship could float if only the front four compartments flooded. But with five damaged compartments, *Titanic* was doomed.

If *Titanic* had hit the iceberg straight on, it might not have sunk. And even if it had sunk, there would have been time for other ships to rescue the people on board.

Illustration showing how *Titanic*'s compartments flooded

Captain Smith knew that *Titanic* had enough lifeboats for 1,178 people—only about half the number of passengers and crew on board. Many people would die if a rescue ship didn't arrive in time.

He rushed to the ship's wireless room and ordered Phillips and Bride to send out distress calls. The first ship to respond was the *Carpathia,* but it was 58 miles away. It would need four hours to reach the sinking ship.

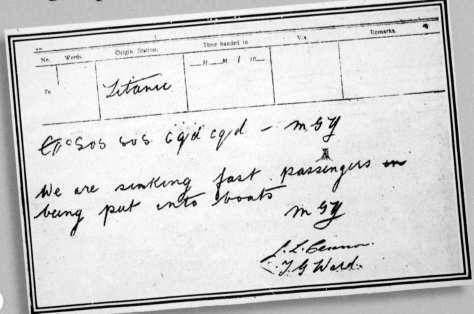

Titanic's crew fired rockets to get the attention of a ship they could see about ten miles away. But it never answered.

weird but true

The original plans for *Titanic* included 64 lifeboats. But the builders put in only 20, so first-class passengers would have more room to stroll around on deck.

The Final Hours

TRAPPED!

First-class passengers had the best chance of getting seats in the lifeboats. Because their rooms were on the upper decks, they could get to the lifeboats more quickly and easily. Many third-class passengers were trapped below decks.

12:25 A.M.

People begin boarding lifeboats, using the code of the sea: "women and children first."

12:45 A.M.

The first lifeboat is lowered into the water. Only 28 of the 65 seats are filled.

In Her Own Words

"We have been living together for many years, and where you go, I go. We started together and if need be, we'll finish together."

—*Ida Straus, overheard speaking to her husband when she decided to die with him rather than board a lifeboat*

The lifeboats were ready by 12:25 a.m., but many people didn't want to board them.

Climbing into the boats was scary. Many passengers couldn't believe that the wonder ship would soon be gone.

The crew worried that they wouldn't have time to lower all the lifeboats, so some boats went down less than half full.

1:15 A.M.

As *Titanic*'s bow sinks, the stern rises out of the water. Lifeboats now leave the ship more fully loaded.

2:05 A.M.

The last lifeboat launches.

2:17 A.M.

People in lifeboats hear a loud crash as everything aboard *Titanic* tumbles toward the bow.

When the last lifeboat launched, more than 1,500 people were stranded on the sinking ship.

As *Titanic*'s stern tilted upward, hundreds of victims fell into the icy water. Others held on until the ship slipped below the waves.

People in the lifeboats were haunted by the victims' desperate screams for help. Then the sounds slowly faded.

In His Own Words

"The lights suddenly went out . . . Slowly [the] stern reared itself up . . . Then with an ever-quickening glide, she slid beneath the water of the cold Atlantic."

—*Second Officer Herbert Lightoller*

2:18 A.M.

The ship's lights go out, the ship breaks into two pieces, and the entire bow sinks.

2:20 A.M.

The stern sinks, leaving hundreds of people in the frigid water.

FREEZING WATERS!

After *Titanic* sank, hundreds of people struggled to survive. That night the ocean was 28° Fahrenheit—a temperature that can cause death in 15 minutes.

3:00 A.M.

A few lifeboats search for survivors. They rescue 13 people.

3:30 A.M.

The survivors see rockets firing in the distance. The *Carpathia* is coming!

They Survived!

A lifeboat approaching *Carpathia*

Many people in the lifeboats were wearing their pajamas. After spending hours in the freezing cold, the *Carpathia* was a welcome sight.

Carpathia's Captain Arthur Rostron

Survivors on board *Carpathia*

Carpathia's crew had plenty of clothes, blankets, and warm food ready for the survivors. They quickly helped the freezing people out of the little lifeboats.

By 9:00 a.m. on Monday, April 15, 1912, *Carpathia* was headed for New York with 705 survivors.

NEVER AGAIN!

After the *Titanic* tragedy, all ships had to have enough lifeboats for everyone on board. A new International Ice Patrol began tracking icebergs and warning nearby ships.

A Real Heroine

One of *Titanic*'s most famous survivors was first-class passenger **Margaret Brown**. She earned the name "Unsinkable Molly Brown" for helping people board lifeboats and insisting that her lifeboat try to rescue people in the water. She may have also taken a turn rowing her lifeboat toward *Carpathia*.

A Careful Observer

First-class passenger **Jack Thayer** was 17 years old—too old to be allowed on a lifeboat. He jumped into the water as *Titanic* sank and scrambled onto an overturned lifeboat. In 1940, Thayer wrote a vivid description of his *Titanic* experience. Robert Ballard used some of Thayer's details to find the sunken ship.

A Hard Worker

Wireless operator **Harold Bride** stayed at his post until the last second. After jumping off the sinking ship, he managed to climb onto the same overturned lifeboat as Jack Thayer. Even though his feet were badly frostbitten, he later helped *Carpathia*'s wireless operator send out survivor lists and personal messages.

The Final Survivor

Third-class passenger **Millvina Dean** was the youngest person aboard *Titanic*. The tiny three-month-old, her two-year-old brother, and her mom were loaded into a lifeboat, but her father went down with the ship. Millvina was the last remaining *Titanic* survivor. She died in 2009.

White Star Line flag

Who Died?

FIRST CLASS
Total: 329
Number who survived: 199
Number who died: 130
40 percent died

SECOND CLASS
Total: 285
Number who survived: 119
Number who died: 166
58 percent died

THIRD CLASS
Total: 715
Number who survived: 179
Number who died: 536
75 percent died

THE CREW
Total: 899
Number who survived: 214
Number who died: 685
76 percent died

News of the disaster spread quickly. No one could believe it. The ship people said was unsinkable had vanished below the waves. And more than 1,500 passengers and crew had suffered a terrible death.

The *Titanic*'s tragic ending made the wonder ship even more famous. Over the years, dozens of books, films, songs, and musicals have retold the shocking story. Even though the ship is long gone, our fascination with it lives on.

The 1997 film *Titanic* is the most successful movie of all time. In two years, it earned nearly $2 billion and won 11 Oscars, including best picture and best director.

10 Real Reasons for the Titanic Tragedy

A hulking iceberg in the middle of the North Atlantic always gets blamed for sinking *Titanic*. But it's not the only reason so many people lost their lives that night.

Illustration of water pouring onto the grand staircase

1 *Titanic*'s builders removed some of the ship's lifeboats, so first-class passengers would have more room on deck. That decision left more than 1,000 people trapped on board the sinking ship.

2 The builders lowered *Titanic*'s bulkheads to make more room for the grand staircase and other fancy features. If the bulkheads had been higher, the ship would have sunk more slowly.

3 *Titanic*'s bow was stronger than the sides of the hull. If the ship had hit the iceberg head on, it might not have sunk.

4 When *Titanic* scraped against the iceberg, the nail-like rivets used to attach the ship's metal sides to the frame broke. As the hull split open, seawater poured into the ship.

5 *Titanic*'s original launch date was March 20, 1912. If the ship had left then, the iceberg probably wouldn't have been in its path.

6 The sea was unusually calm on April 14, 1912. Waves would have made the iceberg easier to spot.

7 *Titanic*'s crew couldn't find the ship's binoculars, so lookout Frederick Fleet was searching for icebergs with just his eyes.

8 Jack Phillips and Harold Bride worked for the company that owned the wireless equipment. If they had worked for the shipping company, they would have known messages about icebergs were more important.

9 Captain Smith delayed his decision to change the ship's course. If he had given the order sooner, the ship would not have been heading in the direction of the iceberg.

10 The *Californian* was just ten miles away. If its wireless radio hadn't been turned off for the night, the ship could have saved people before *Titanic* sank.

Search and Discovery

For more than 70 years, no human eyes saw *Titanic*. Many people tried to find the ship, but they failed.

weird but true

Titanic was found more than 13 miles from its last reported location. No wonder people had such a hard time finding it!

All that changed in 1985. That's when Robert Ballard used *Argo*—a new kind of underwater vehicle—to locate the trail of broken pieces that fell out of *Titanic* as it sank. Then he followed this trail of remains to the ship.

In 1986, Ballard visited the sunken ship in a tiny submarine. It landed on *Titanic*'s deck and sent a robot named *J.J.* inside to look around.

Robert Ballard called *J.J.* a "swimming eyeball."

Titanic Treasures

When Robert Ballard announced *Titanic*'s location in 1986, people began to visit the site. They all wanted to see the wonder ship. And many wanted to take pieces of it home. People have removed more than 6,000 items from *Titanic*.

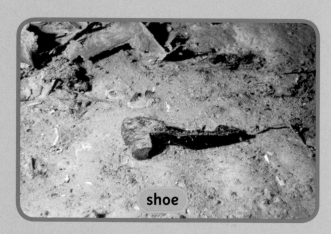
shoe

WHAT DO YOU THINK?

Robert Ballard thinks people should leave *Titanic* alone. He says that taking things—dishes, lamps, pieces of the ship—is like robbing a grave.

Human bodies and clothing decay quickly in seawater, but shoes don't. A shoe marks a *Titanic* victim's final resting place.

Rusticles cover a first-class cabin of *Titanic*.

Over time, visitors have damaged *Titanic*. So have tiny ocean creatures. Reddish brown rusticles now cover most of the ship. They form as bacteria and fungi dine on iron and steel.

Titanic Terms

RUSTICLES: A form of rust- and metal-eating bacteria and fungi

Submarines like this one were used to survey the *Titanic* wreck for the 3-D model.

WHY?

Why do scientists want to make a detailed computer model of *Titanic*? Because someday that's all that will be left of the wonder ship.

In 2010, scientists spent 20 days photographing and filming every inch of *Titanic,* including its huge trail of broken pieces. The images will be used to create a 3-D model of the site.

You'll probably never visit *Titanic* in person, but soon, you'll be able to explore the shipwreck virtually from the comfort of your living room. How cool is that?

One of *Titanic*'s propellers

The top of an engine

Glossary

BRIDGE: A ship's control center. *Titanic* was steered and navigated from its bridge.

ICEBERG: A large mass of ice floating in the sea

HULL: The lowest part of a ship, partly covered with water

TRAGIC: Sad, dreadful, disastrous

RUSTICLES: A form of rust- and metal-eating bacteria and fungi

BOW: The front end of a ship

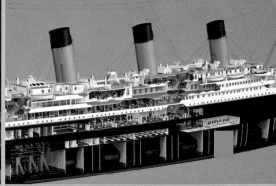

BULKHEADS: Walls meant to slow or prevent flooding by separating *Titanic's* hull into 16 separate compartments

IMMIGRANTS: People who leave one country to settle in another country

LUXURY: Something that offers pleasure or comfort, but isn't necessary; often difficult or expensive to get

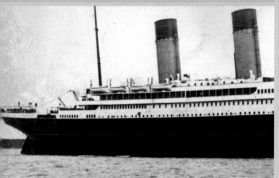

STERN: The back end of a ship

WIRELESS: An early form of radio that relayed messages through a coded series of beeps

Index

Boldface indicates illustrations.